Mixing it up with ...

Harry Potter

Also available in the same series:

Owen Smith, *Mixing it up with ... Football*
Owen Smith, *Mixing it up with ... The Simpsons*

Mixing it up with . . .

Harry Potter

12 sessions about faith for 9–13s

Owen Smith

CHURCH HOUSE
PUBLISHING

Church House Publishing
Church House
Great Smith Street
London SW1P 3AZ
Tel: 020 7898 1451
Fax: 020 7898 1449

ISBN 978-0-7151-4106-9

Published 2007 by Church House Publishing.

Cover design by www.penquinboy.net
Printed in England by Halstan and Co. Ltd, Amersham, Bucks

Contents

Introduction

How this book came about

Six months after I started work at St Margaret's Church, Rainham, I carried out a review of all our work with young people, to identify which groups we were working with and which we were failing to have any contact with. As part of that review, it became clear that there were certain gaps in our provision. One such gap was suitable provision for the ten- and eleven-year-old boys who were too young to come along to the church youth group, and who either found that the style of the Sunday morning provision we had at the time didn't cater to their interests, or were unable to come on Sunday because of football matches and other commitments. We identified some boys who came from families within the congregation, and some who were known to us through outreach projects we had recently run in the local community, and invited them to a midweek group, later dubbed 'Superb'. As I looked round for material aimed at the 9–13 age group, I found that there was very little available and even less that capitalized on the interests of young people of this age.

With this in mind, I set about writing some material that used examples of the culture in which these young people are immersed to introduce and explore relevant Christian themes. These sessions are the result!

Who is this material for?

A recent study found that more young people stopped coming to church at the age of eleven than at any other age,[1] yet this is an age group which is largely under-resourced by churches. Therefore, this material is aimed at young people aged nine to thirteen. It is suitable both for young people who already have some church involvement and for those on the fringe, who may find it too difficult to come to other church activities for cultural reasons or because the times of regular church groups are inconvenient.

As the activities do not require a huge amount of space, this material is suitable for use with midweek groups, a Sunday school, or a school lunchtime group. Each session lasts about 45 minutes, but the length can be tailored to suit your individual setting. Forty-five minutes is only enough to provide an introduction to a topic. Therefore, if in the course of the sessions you find that a certain issue or question is of particular interest to your young people, you can go back to it and cover it in greater depth at a later date.

Working with nine- to thirteen-year-olds

Young people aged between nine and thirteen years of age are undergoing a huge number of changes – both physically and mentally. They are about to embark on the often treacherous journey through adolescence, and they are beginning to know their own mind. They are moving away from their parents towards their peers and are beginning to develop the sense of self which they'll carry with them into their adult lives.[2] They have a new-found capacity for abstract thought and can now consider a variety of opinions and possible outcomes, thinking through situations without needing concrete experiences.[3] All this means that groups and activities for this age group should differ from those aimed at younger children or teenagers.

Setting up a group

When setting up a group for young people of this age, there are a number of things it's important to consider. Firstly, you need to decide who your group is aimed at. The material in these sessions is more suitable for those young people with some existing knowledge of Christian teaching, and would therefore work well for a group that seeks to nurture and encourage the young people who are already part of the church community, or who are wishing to explore more of what the Christian faith has to say about some important questions. Secondly, you might also want to think about whether your young people would feel more comfortable meeting in a single-sex group. This will depend on the personalities and the gender breakdown of the young people you are aiming at.

When to hold your group

You need to identify the best time for your group to meet. It might be that you use this material with a group as part of your provision for children and young people on a Sunday morning. However, you might find, as we did, that Sunday is not a good time for them to come to a group such as this. Thankfully we are moving away from the idea that church and worship only take place on a Sunday, and it may be that your work with this age group needs a 'fresh expression' of church. For more about such groups and initiatives, have a look at the fresh expressions website – http://www.freshexpressions.org.uk As many young people play sports or have other commitments on a Sunday morning, we found that a midweek session fitted in far better with all the other activities they were involved in.

Venue

As well as the 'when', it's also important to have thought through the 'where' of your group. The venue for your sessions is very important in determining how your group will run. It may be that you have very limited options over where you can meet, but the environment can have a huge impact on how a session goes. You need a room big enough to allow your group to relax in comfort and free of major distractions. You will also need a television and a DVD player. Possible venues might include the home of a member of the group, the vicarage (as long as you've asked the vicar first!), or the church hall. Wherever you decide to meet, you must make sure that you are following the child protection guidelines set by your church or organization – more about this below.

Ground rules

As you begin to meet as a group, you may find it useful to ask the group members to come up with some kind of agreement about how the group will work. Obviously you don't want it to feel like school, but it is often good to get your young people to come up with a few basic ground rules that set out what is expected of each member of the group, including you, and what behaviour is not acceptable to the group during a session. These rules might include the group's thoughts about how they should treat each other and how they should treat the place in which you meet. They could also include some rules to make sure that your group is a 'safe' environment where everyone feels able to contribute to the discussions. Such rules might include keeping within the group the things members share during sessions, rather than talking about them to other friends afterwards, and making sure that everyone gets a chance to say what they think without being interrupted.

Group identity

Establishing a strong group identity and a sense of ownership of the group is essential when working with 9–13s. These young people are at a point in their lives when 'belonging' is very important. We need to be careful not to establish cliques, but making your group one to which the young people feel attached can be an important part of maintaining their interest, particularly as they make the transition from primary to secondary education. I got the young people to come up with a name for their group during the first session. Introducing regular occurrences unique to the group can help to bond the young people and strengthen the group. These might be simple things like always having doughnuts when it's someone's birthday, having some sort of reward if a group member brings their own Bible to session, or giving a prize to the first person to find the Bible passage.

Good practice: child protection and health and safety

It is important that you make yourself aware of the guidelines your organization has in place to protect you as a leader, and the young people you are working with. These will probably take the form of a child protection policy and good practice guidelines, and will be available from your Diocesan Children's or Youth Officer, or equivalent. Making yourself aware of these guidelines is a key part of preparing yourself to run a group. On the basis of these guidelines, you will need to consider how many leaders your group will need to have present when it meets. For young people aged eight and over, the normal ratio is one leader for every eight young people, with a minimum of two leaders.

You will also need to consider what contact information and parental permission you need to seek from the young people who will attend your group. For more information on matters relating to child protection and best practice, get in touch with your Diocesan Children's or Youth Officer, or your church's equivalent, who will be happy to give you further advice.

Handling sensitive issues

Some of the sessions in this book cover topics that might bring up issues that will be sensitive for particular members of the group. Talking about things such as families, or self-image, might raise both positive and negative anxieties, memories and experiences. If a young person shares such feelings, it may be appropriate to talk them through as part of the discussion during the session – young people are often surprisingly mature when it appears that a member of their group is hurting. However, sometimes it might be better to gently suggest that you talk to the young person at a more suitable time. Be careful not to diminish the importance of what they have or want to share, but explain that it might be something that is better talked about in a more suitable setting. If at any point you feel that you are getting out of your depth – don't keep going! It may be that you need to talk to your vicar or line manager about getting help from someone with more experience in dealing with such issues. You don't have to know all the answers, but knowing where to find out more is a good start!

Encouraging your group to talk

Some of the activities included within the sessions involve discussion, and this might prove difficult for some groups. Some young people will feed off one another's ideas and will be able to hold interesting and lively discussions. In groups such as this, make sure that one or two key people aren't monopolizing the discussion. You might need to draw in the quieter members of the group, gently inviting them to contribute, remembering that they might not want to say anything! If the discussion becomes too rowdy, you might need to pause for a moment and make sure that members take turns to contribute their opinions.

When faced with a question for discussion, other groups will sit in silence, avoiding eye contact with anyone in the room. Initially, don't worry about silence – it might just take a moment for the young people to process what you are asking. However, if the silence persists, you may need to restate the question, breaking it down into simpler ideas. Use open questions to stimulate the discussion – questions that can't simply be answered by a 'yes' or a 'no'. Sometimes, it may work better to ask the group to discuss a particular issue from the point of view of a third party within a scenario. Some groups will find it much easier to talk about how 'David' or 'Helen' might feel or act in a certain situation, rather than how they themselves would feel or act.

To help the person leading the session, we've provided possible answers for each of the questions asked (indicated in brackets after the question). However, ideally you want your young people to discuss the issues that are raised, engaging with each topic, rather than just providing you with what they think is the right answer. Young people who have been involved in the church's children and youth provision since an early age will know what they think the right answer should be, and will give it with ease. However, your job as facilitator is to encourage them to go deeper than the 'right answer' and talk about what they actually think and believe – do they agree with the right answer, what are the problems with the right answer, what questions does the 'right answer' leave us with?

Why use contemporary culture?

Using the culture of the day to help engage people in thinking about Christian themes is not a new idea! When Jesus taught the people he met on his travels, he used stories and illustrations firmly rooted in the culture of the time. The parables he used to convey his messages were often based on agricultural or social scenarios, with which his audience would have been able to identify.

In the past, the Church has sometimes appeared more wary of the ever-expanding influence that media such as television and film have on people, sometimes perceiving them more as a threat than an aid. Today, young people coming to the end of primary school and starting secondary education are immersed in a culture of satellite TV, Playstations, celebrities, *Big Brother* and footballers. It is a culture where 'anything goes' and 'want it *NOW*' seem to be the prevailing philosophies. In order to engage with these young people we need to use the heroes and images they encounter daily to explore what are often, to them, unfamiliar Christian themes.

The idea of using contemporary culture to introduce and explore Christian themes is one that can be applied to many different sources. If you have a group whose interests lie more in music than Harry Potter, then using lyrics from their favourite songs as the basis for a session might be an excellent way to engage them in thinking about these themes. You might want to look at resources such as *Music to Move the Soul*[4] for examples of such material. *Youthwork Magazine* (www.youthwork.co.uk) has regular features showing how different aspects of youth culture can be used in this way.

The Internet is an amazing tool for developing such sessions – you can find episode summaries, plot synopses, quotations from films, and lyrics for songs, as well as a wealth of background material and trivia.

Why use Harry Potter?

As of February 2007, the 2001 film version of J. K. Rowling's *Harry Potter and the Philosopher's Stone* has taken over £66 million through UK box offices alone – the highest amount ever taken by a UK film.[5] To date, over 300 million copies of Harry Potter books have been sold worldwide, translated into over 63 languages.[6] Statistics like these, and many more, begin to reveal the magnitude of the Harry Potter phenomenon. J. K. Rowling published the first instalment of the Harry Potter saga in 1997. Popularity has grown as the seven books, which tell the story of Harry's adventures at Hogwarts, have been released, with the final one published in July 2007. So far, the first five books have been turned into films (*Harry Potter and the Philosopher's Stone* in 2001, *Harry Potter and the Chamber of Secrets* in 2002, *Harry Potter and the Prisoner of Azkaban* in 2004, *Harry Potter and the Goblet of Fire* in 2005, and *Harry Potter and the Order of the Phoenix* in 2007), with the remaining two (*Harry Potter and the Half-blood Prince* and *Harry Potter and the Deathly Hallows*) to be made and released over the next few years.

Since 1997, much has been written about the effects these books, and later the films, have had on children and adults alike. In the Christian world, much of the discussion has centred around whether Christians should be reading these books and, more importantly, whether we should let our children engage with the world of Harry and Hogwarts. Whether we like it or not, J. K. Rowling's books, and the subsequent films, have become a major part of the culture in which our young people live. So should we be allowing these books and films to feature within our ministries? In short, the answer is yes. When Christians start to alienate themselves from what is happening in the real world, they begin to become islands – islands that are viewed by the majority of people as weird, or worse. God has called us to lead lives that are distinct in character, but which might not require us to shut ourselves off from everything that is not inherently religious in character.

Others have asked whether it is appropriate to draw Christian themes from stories that are obviously not Christian in origin. In answer to this concern, I think it should be clear that these sessions do not build upon the Christian elements of the Harry Potter stories, as the author has never claimed that these elements exist.[7] Instead, these sessions draw parallels between events in the world of Harry and his friends, and the world in which we are seeking to proclaim the gospel to our young people. These parallels allow our young people to access more easily some complex Christian concepts, by bridging their understanding of Harry Potter to their understanding of the Christian faith.

Finally, some have voiced the worry that Harry Potter will lead our young people towards the occult – that by reading these books and watching these films they will be drawn into a world of dark magic and occult horror. I disagree. The magic in the books is simply a part of the world that J. K. Rowling has created, in the same way that magic is part of the world of Christian writers such as C. S. Lewis and J. R. R. Tolkein, and often a part of the imaginary world in which children play.[8] To say, as some have, that these books draw younger readers towards the occult seems to me both to malign J. K. Rowling and to vastly underestimate the ability of children and young people to separate the real from the imaginary.

There isn't enough time or space here to fully engage with the debate surrounding Harry Potter, but there is a wealth of writing available that deals with the subject in more depth. To find out more, look at the range of books available from Church House Bookshop, by visiting their web site: http://www.chbookshop.co.uk/feature.asp?id=2387220

Caution!

However, there will always be elements of popular culture that are not, as Paul said, as good, as pure or as admirable as we would like (Philippians 4.8). It is part of our responsibility to make it clear to our young people that there are aspects of the culture in which we live that are good and to be encouraged, and aspects that we need to be more wary of. Christians cannot establish themselves as islands, detached from the culture that permeates all areas of our lives – Jesus called us to be in the world, but not of it. We need to equip our young people with the ability to discern those things that are not acceptable, supporting them as they form their opinions of the world around them. During the sessions you might want to mention some of the less admirable aspects of Harry Potter as they arise, challenging the group over their thoughts about them.

Using film clips

Using film clips as part of any teaching session or church service is an excellent way to get people of all ages to think about a particular theme. However, when doing so, there are a couple of things that need to be noted. First, you need to make sure that the clip or film you are showing is suitable. Film Classification Certificates (e.g. U, PG, 12, etc.) give a reliable indicator of whether or not a film is suitable for a certain age group. However, there may be occasions when you decide to use a short clip that is suitable for a particular age group, even though the rest of the film isn't. The first three films are certificate PG, while the fourth film, *Harry Potter and the Goblet of Fire,* is certificate 12. However, all the clips used in these sessions are suitable for those members of the group under twelve, and conform to the standards laid out by the British Board of Film Classification for a PG certificate film. More information about film classifications can be found on the BBFC website (http://www.bbfc.co.uk).

The other issue you need to look at is whether your church has the appropriate licences to show films as part of services or small group teaching sessions. For detailed information on this subject, contact Christian Copyright Licensing International (CCLI), on 01323 436103, or via their website (http://www.ccli.co.uk/) and ask about church video licences.

The shape of this material

This book contains twelve sessions. Each session is designed to last just under an hour and includes the following:

Beforehand . . . This tells the person leading the group about any preparation that will need to be done before you start the session.

Opening activity . . . This activity introduces the session's theme and aims to get the young people thinking about the issue. It is usually quite short, and should last between 5 and 15 minutes.

Film clip . . . A short clip from one of the first four Harry Potter films, which provides a starting point to begin to discuss the session's theme.

Taking it further . . . This activity then develops the theme, allowing the young people to explore what they think about it in greater depth.

Bible focus . . . The young people then look up a Bible verse or passage that deals with the Christian perspective on the session's theme. Here the verses are quoted from the NIV, but you might want to use a different version if that's what your group is used to.

Prayer response . . . Each session then ends with a prayer activity drawing on the session's theme, and giving the young people a chance to respond in some way.

Thanks

The writing of this book has involved the patience of a lot of people, to all of whom I owe a great deal! I'd like to thank my Superb cell group (Ross, Alex, Tom, Jack, Joe, Connor, Craig, John, David, Fenner and Nick) for helping me refine the sessions and telling me what they thought with no holds barred! My thanks also go to my boss Canon Alan Vousden for enduring my constant mess in his nice clean office, and to our wonderful Rochester Diocesan Youth Adviser Phil Greig for making me think about publishing these sessions in the first place.

Notes

1   Peter Brierley, *Reaching and Keeping Tweenagers*, Christian Research Association.
2   Erik H. Erikson, *Identity: Youth and Crisis*, W. W. Norton, 1968.
3   Jean Piaget (translated by W. Mays), *The Principles of Genetic Epistemology*, Routledge, 1972.
4   Steve and Ruth Adams, *Music to Move the Soul*, Spring Harvest, 2003.
5   http://www.bfi.org.uk/filmtvinfo/stats/boxoffice/10ukfilms.html
6   http://news.bbc.co.uk/1/hi/entertainment/arts/4308548.stm
7   Philip Plyming, *Harry Potter and the Meaning of Life*, Grove Books Ltd, 2001.
8   Dr. Jerram Barrs, *J.K. Rowling and Harry Potter*, http://www.bethinking.org, 2004.

SESSION AIM........ **To understand that God loves us as his children**

QUOTATION.......... **Hagrid:** You're a wizard Harry.
Harry: I'm a what?
Hagrid: A wizard. And a thumpin' good one I'd wager once you've trained up a bit.
Harry: No, you've made a mistake. I mean I can't be a wizard. I mean I'm Harry. Just Harry.

FILM FOCUS......... *Harry Potter and the Philosopher's Stone*, chapter 4 (time code: 00:11:47), ending when Hagrid gives Harry the letter (time code: 00:15:08). (Duration: 3:21)

BIBLE FOCUS........ 'How great is the love the Father has lavished on us, that we should be called children of God! And that is what we are!' (1 John 3.1)

RESOURCES.......... *Post-it notes*, Philosopher's Stone *DVD, paper, pens, Bible, playdough*

- Prepare Post-it notes ready for the first activity by writing the names of famous people from current news, films, sport and cartoons on enough Post-it notes for one for each group member.

Who's who
(10 minutes)
This session begins with a very traditional game. Take the Post-it notes you have prepared and stick one on the forehead (or back if they'd prefer) of each group member, without letting them see what it says. Members of the group have to guess who they are by going round the room and asking other people questions that can only be answered with 'yes' or 'no'. The aim is to find out the name written on their Post-it note. Watch out for cheating!

(10 minutes)
Explain that during this session we are going to be thinking about the question 'Who am I?' It's a difficult, complicated question to ask ourselves, and one that we'll have to think about all through our lives. We're going to start by watching a clip from *Harry Potter and the Philosopher's Stone*, in which Harry finds out an answer to that question. Get the group to think about the following questions:

- How does Harry find out that he's a wizard? (Hagrid comes to the place where he is staying to tell him.)
- How does he react to the news? (He is amazed!)
- Why doesn't he think he can be a wizard? (Harry doesn't think he is anything special.)

Who are you?

(15 minutes)

Give each member of the group a piece of paper and a pen. Invite each person to draw a rough picture of themselves in the middle of the paper. Once they've done that, get them to write words round their picture that they think describe them. They might choose words that describe what they look like, words that describe their personality, or words that describe their skills, talents or hobbies. Get willing group members to share what they have written with the rest of the group.

on Bible passage

Bible focus

(10 minutes)

We can all answer the question 'Who am I?' in a number of different ways – we can talk about 'who we are' in terms of how we look, how we act, what we are good at, where we live or what we like to eat. However, the Bible gives some different answers to the question 'Who am I?', one of which can be found in 1 John 3.1.

- Who (or what) does this verse say we are? (We are children of God.)
- What does this tell us about how God thinks about us? (He loves us and cares for us in the way that a parent cares about their child.)
- How do the young people think that a good parent should look after their child? (Feed them, clothe them, guide them, protect them, etc.)
- How does this relate to how God looks after us?

response

Thank you for making me ME

(10 minutes)

Each one of us has been created as one of God's children – unique and special. God loves us just as we are. To help the young people think about this, give each of them a piece of playdough. Give them some time to make a model or representation of something that is unique about them – they might choose to represent one of the ways they described themselves earlier in the session, or a skill or talent they have, or something about the way they look. Encourage them to choose something they are proud of. Once everyone has made their model, go round the group and encourage each person to thank God for making them unique in the way they have chosen. If your group are reluctant to pray out loud, get each person to use the pattern 'Dear God thank you for making me . . .'. Once everyone has prayed, end the session with a short prayer thanking God for making us his children. You could use one of your own or the prayer below.

PLATFORM
9 3/4

Dear God,
Thank you that you have made each one of us unique,
  and have called us your children.
Help us to remember that we are all special to you.
Amen.

2 what do you want?

SESSION AIM........ **To think about focusing on what God wants rather than on what we want**

QUOTATION.......... **Dumbledore:** It shows nothing more or less than the deepest and most desperate desires of our hearts . . . This mirror gives us neither knowledge nor truth. It does not do to dwell on dreams and forget to live.

FILM FOCUS......... *Harry Potter and the Philosopher's Stone*, chapter 23 (time code: 1:27:57), ending when we see Harry in the snow (time code: 1:32:44). (Duration: 4:47)

BIBLE FOCUS........ 'He has showed you, O man, what is good. And what does the LORD require of you? To act justly and to love mercy and to walk humbly with your God.' (Micah 6.8)

RESOURCES.......... *Pictures of both celebrities and ordinary people, Philosopher's Stone DVD, paper, pens, Bible, two bowls, copies of cards*

BEFOREHAND

- Find pictures of people (both celebrities and ordinary people), either off the Internet or from newspapers and magazines.
- Photocopy the sheet on page 6 and cut out and fold up the cards so that there are enough to give one to each person.

OPENING activity

Want want want
(10 minutes)

Begin by asking the young people to sit themselves in a circle. This game works in the same way as the shopping list game. Choose a member of the group to begin the game by completing the sentence 'I really really really want . . .'. The person on their right then completes the sentence with their own answer, then adds the previous person's answer to the end of their own. The next person round the circle then completes the sentence, adding the second and the first person's answer to the end of their own. As the game progresses, each person has to add their own ending to the sentence and remember, in order, each answer given by previous members of the group. The winner of the game is the person who can successfully remember the most items in a row. What do your young people really really really want?

FILM CLIP

(10 minutes)

Watch the clip for this session and get your group to think about the following questions:
- What does Dumbledore tell Harry the mirror of Erised does? (It shows what the person looking into it wants most in the world.)

- What does Harry want? (Harry wants his parents to be alive and proud of him.)
- What does Ron want? (He wants to be head boy, win the Quidditch Cup, be Quidditch Captain and look good.)
- Why does Dumbledore have the mirror moved? (Because people have wasted their lives or gone mad thinking about what it shows, rather than living their lives.)

What do they want?

(10 minutes)

Divide the young people into small groups. Give each group a variety of pictures of people, either printed off the Internet or taken from newspapers and magazines. These people should be pop stars, TV stars, sports stars and ordinary people. Working in these groups, get the young people to come up with a list of ideas of what these celebrities might want – what sorts of things are they aiming for, or working towards being able to do or afford? Once they've come up with a list, get them to add possible explanations for these desires – why do people desire money, or girlfriends, or cars or popularity? Feed back the young people's answers to the rest of the group.

on Bible passage

Bible focus

(10 minutes)

Often people are very good at knowing what they want, whether it's the latest game, or the latest make of trainers, but how good are we at knowing what God wants. Get the group to look up Micah 6.8 and think about the following questions:

- What does God want us to do? (He wants us to act justly, love mercy, and walk humbly with him.)
- What do each of these things mean? (To act justly is to be fair to those around us, to love mercy is to be forgiving to those around us, and to walk humbly is to depend on God, knowing that we can't do a thing by our own strength alone.)
- Why does God want these things? (Because God knows that these things are the things that will give us the best possible life.)
- Why do you think he might let us choose to do these things rather than make us do them? (Because God prefers his people to act out of love for him rather than because they have to.)
- Can the group think of examples of how they might do what God wants during their day-to-day lives?

response

Swap it!

(10 minutes)

Place two bowls in the middle of the circle, one of which contains the pieces of paper you prepared before the session. Explain to the young people that it can be all too easy for what we want and desire to get in the way of what God wants, even though what God wants for us will be better than what we want for ourselves. Give each young person a piece of paper and a pen, and give them some time to think about something they want which they think might be getting in the way of them doing what God wants. Maybe their desire for the latest console, or their desire to be liked by the people in their class is stopping them living as God wants. Once the young people have had time to write something on their pieces of paper, invite them one by one to come up, and place their piece of paper in the empty bowl in the middle of the circle, and take one of the pieces of paper in the other bowl. Finish the session with a prayer, either one of your own or using the one below:

PLATFORM 9¾

Dear God,
Thank you for knowing what is best for us,
 even when we think we know what we want.
Help us to act justly, to love mercy and to walk humbly with you.
Amen.

Encourage the young people to take the piece of paper they chose home with them, and to think about how they can do what God wants this week.

Photocopy these onto paper or card and cut them up ready for use during the session.

Act Justly

This week, share something that you own with someone else.

Walk Humbly

Tell God about something you are really finding difficult at the moment.

Love Mercy

Forgive someone who is really annoying you this week.

Act Justly

Lend a helping hand to someone you live with.

Walk Humbly

Tell God about something you are really finding difficult at the moment.

Love Mercy

Don't get angry and shout at someone, even though they deserve it.

Act Justly

Lend a helping hand to someone you live with.

Walk Humbly

Spend some time every day thanking God for the good things he has done for you.

Love Mercy

Help someone out of a difficult situation they've got themselves into this week

Love Mercy

Forgive yourself – let go of anything you are still beating yourself up about.

Act Justly

Help someone who doesn't have as much as you.

Walk Humbly

Set aside 15 minutes to sit and do nothing but listen to what God is saying to you.

3 Love on show . . .

SESSION AIM........	**To understand the nature and importance of love**
QUOTATION..........	**Dumbledore:** Harry, do you know why Professor Quirrell couldn't bear to have you touch him? It was because of your mother. She sacrificed herself for you. And that kind of act leaves a mark. No, no this kind of mark cannot be seen. It lives in your very skin.
	Harry: What is it?
	Dumbledore: Love, Harry. Love.
FILM FOCUS.........	*Harry Potter and the Philosopher's Stone*, chapter 32 (time code: 2:08:48), ending when Dumbledore says 'Alas, Earwax' (time code: 2:11:48). (Duration: 3:00)
BIBLE FOCUS........	'Love is patient, love is kind. It does not envy, it does not boast, it is not proud. It is not rude, it is not self-seeking, it is not easily angered, it keeps no record of wrongs. Love does not delight in evil but rejoices with the truth. It always protects, always trusts, always hopes, always perseveres.' (1 Corinthians 13.4-7)
RESOURCES..........	Philosopher's Stone *DVD, paper hearts, Bible, pipe-cleaners, A5 paper, Sellotape.*

- Photocopy and cut out the paper hearts for use later in the session.

All you need is . . .
(5 minutes)

Begin the session with a game of charades. Choose a member of the group and show them one of the items from the list below (or a list of your own creation). Explain to the group that your volunteer is going to mime (with no noise at all!) the title of a song or film that has the word 'love' in it. Get the group to guess the title of the film or song. Suitable titles include:

- 'Love is all around (I feel it in my fingers)'
- 'I will always love you'
- *Shakespeare in Love*
- *The Spy who loved me*
- 'How deep is your love?'
- *Love Actually*
- *From Russia with Love*

(10 minutes)

Watch the film clip from *Harry Potter and the Philosopher's Stone*. Get the group to discuss the following questions arising from what they've seen:

- What kind of mark did Dumbledore say Harry had? (A mark on the inside, not a physical mark.)
- What had left its mark on him? (Love)
- How had his mother shown this love to Harry? (She'd given up her own life to save him.)

What's love got to do with it?
(10 minutes)

Love can be a difficult idea to get your head round. It's used in films, songs, adverts and more. But how do your young people recognize love – what does love look like? Hand out the paper hearts and pens to each member of the group. Give them some time to think about how people show love? Explain that Harry's mother showed her love by the sacrifice she made for Harry, but how do we see people showing love to each other? How do we know what love looks like? Get them to write the ideas they come up with on their hearts. Collect up the hearts, mix them up, and then get each member to randomly choose one and read out what's written on it. Does the group agree with that idea – is it a way they think people demonstrate love?

on Bible passage

Bible focus
(10 minutes)

Get the young people to look up one of the Bible's descriptions of what love looks like in 1 Corinthians, and have a look at the following questions:

- How does Paul describe love – what does he say love is like? (Patient, kind, not envious, not boastful, not proud, not rude, not self-seeking. It protects, hopes, trusts and perseveres.)
- The Bible tells us to love all sorts of people. Can the young people think of who we are told to love? (God, ourselves, our neighbours and our enemies.)
- Can the young people think of examples of how we might show a love like this towards these people? How could we be patient or kind or trustworthy, etc. towards ourselves, towards our neighbours, or towards our enemies?

response

Love is all around
(10 min)

The question this leaves us with is: how can we show this type of love to those around us? Give each young person a pipe-cleaner and a piece of paper. Get them to bend their pipe-cleaner into a heart shape and stick it, using pieces of Sellotape, onto their paper. Ideally their pipe-cleaner heart should have a space in the middle where they can write things. Once everyone has a heart, give the young people time to write a prayer in the middle of their heart, asking God to help them love someone this week. They might choose to love a neighbour – to do something nice for someone they wouldn't normally talk to, or they might choose to love an enemy – to find some way this week of showing God's love to someone they normally don't get on with. They might choose to love a friend, a family member, someone at church – whoever they choose, get them to write a short prayer asking God to help them love this person in some way this week. Once everyone has written their prayer, give them a chance to read out their prayers one after the other. Finish with a prayer of your own or the prayer below.

PLATFORM

Dear God,
Thank you for showing us how much you love us
   by sending us your Son.
Help us to show love to those around us
   by being patient, kind and trusting
rather than being envious, rude and angry.
Amen.

What's love got to do with it?

Photocopy this page onto paper (red or pink if you've got it) and cut them up so you have enough to give each member of the group.

4 It's only words?

SESSION AIM......... **To think about the importance of choosing our words carefully**

QUOTATION.......... **Hermione:** He called me a Mudblood ... It means dirty blood. Mudblood's a really foul name for someone who was Muggle-born. Someone with non-magic parents. Someone like me. It's not a term one usually hears in civilized conversation.

FILM FOCUS......... *Harry Potter and the Chamber of Secrets,* chapter 12 (time code: 0:36:27), ending when Gilderoy Lockhart says 'Harry Harry Harry' (time code: 0:39:54). (Duration: 3:27)

BIBLE FOCUS........ 'If anyone considers himself religious and yet does not keep a tight rein on his tongue, he deceives himself and his religion is worthless.' (James 1.26)

RESOURCES.......... *Three dictionaries, stopwatch, prizes, Chamber of Secrets DVD, paper, pens, Bible, Scrabble letters*

- Words for the first game if you choose to play it this way.
- Photocopy enough copies of the 'For Good or For Bad' worksheet to give one to each pair or group of young people.

Choose 'em carefully ...
(10 minutes)
Give three members of the group a dictionary each, and choose a fourth member of the group to be the first to play this game. Each person with a dictionary is going to open it at a random page and point to a random word. The fourth person then has just 30 seconds to link these three words together in a sentence or short story. If they can link these three words (whether they know what they mean or not) in a creative way within the 30 seconds, give them a prize! Swap around the dictionaries and choose a new player. Continue until everyone who wants to has had a go. Explain that during this session they are going to be thinking about the importance of choosing our words carefully.

If your group will find choosing and reading words from the dictionary too difficult because of their level of literacy, use the words on page 12. Cut up the words and mix them up in a bowl. Each volunteer chooses three without looking and the game then continues, as detailed above, by trying to link the three words in just 30 seconds. Make sure the words are returned to the bowl afterwards, ready for the next player.

(10 minutes)
Watch the clip from *Harry Potter and the Chamber of Secrets* in which we see Hermione being called a rather unpleasant name. Get the group to think about the following questions:
- What did Malfoy call Hermione? (A Mudblood)

- Why did Malfoy call her that? (He thought he was better than her and didn't like the fact that she wasn't a pure-blooded wizard.)
- What effect did it have on Hermione? (She was upset that she had been called Mudblood.)
- How did Hermione's friends react to Malfoy's name-calling? (They were shocked and angry – Ron tried to retaliate.)
- What did Hagrid do to make Hermione feel better? (He told her she was a brilliant student – he used his words to encourage her.)

For good or for bad
(*10 minutes*)

Divide the young people into pairs or small groups. Give each group or pair a copy of the worksheet. On one side, get the young people to suggest ways that words can be used positively (to praise, to encourage, to bless, to congratulate, to admire, etc.). On the other side, get them to list the opposite – ways in which words can be used negatively (to ridicule, to insult, to cuss, to belittle, etc.). Once groups have come up with their two lists, feed them back to the rest of the group. What are some of the ways we can use our words for good and for bad?

FOCUS
on Bible passage

Bible focus
(*10 minutes*)

The Bible talks about how we ought to use our words – get the group to look up James 1.26 and then think about the following questions:
- What does it mean to be 'religious'? (Being people who try and follow what God says rather than what the world says.)
- How can we keep a 'tight rein' on our tongue? (By watching what we say, and using our words for positive rather than negative things.)
- Why does it make one's religion 'worthless'? (Because what you say doesn't match up with what you think and believe, and this might make people around you doubt that you are trying to be like Jesus.)

PRAYER
response

A to Z
(*10 minutes*)

Pass a bag full of Scrabble tiles round the circle. Each person takes a Scrabble tile and then has to pray for something based on the letter they have chosen. They might pray for someone whose name begins with that letter, or say thank you for something they have – they can choose to use their letter in their prayer in any way they like. If your group isn't used to praying out loud, you might need to help them by giving them a model prayer to use such as 'Dear God, thank you for . . .' or 'Dear God, please help . . .', etc. Depending on how your group respond to the activity, go round the circle once or more, then finish with a prayer of your own or the prayer below.

PLATFORM
9 ¾

Dear God,
Help us to think about how we choose our words.
Help us to use what we say to encourage and support those around us.
Amen.

Photocopy this page and cut up into individual words for use in the first activity.

Socks	Wheel
Lemon	Jump
Fork	Crunchy
Laugh	Glass
Green	Cold
Pencil	Teacher
Run	Lion
Ipod	Table
Book	Magazine
Chocolate	Traffic

Working in your pairs or groups, come up with ways that words can be used positively (praise, encourage, etc.) and ways that words can be used negatively (to insult, to cuss, etc.).

Words for GOOD

Words for BAD

5 Boasting

SESSION AIM......... **To think about the things we boast about**

QUOTATION.......... **Snape:** Weren't you saying just last night that you've known all along where the entrance to the Chamber of Secrets is?

FILM FOCUS......... *Harry Potter and the Chamber of Secrets*, chapter 28 (time code 1:46:35), ending when Ron says 'Ginny' (time code 1:50:43). (Duration: 4:08)

BIBLE FOCUS........ 'This is what the LORD says: "Let not the wise man boast of his wisdom or the strong man boast of his strength or the rich man boast of his riches, but let him who boasts boast about this: that he understands and knows me, that I am the LORD, who exercises kindness, justice and righteousness on earth, for in these I delight," declares the LORD.' (Jeremiah 9.23-24)

RESOURCES.......... *Chamber of Secrets* DVD, balloons, felt-tip pens, Bible, Post-it notes, large sheet of paper.

- Prepare the large sheet of paper for use in the prayer activity by writing on it the word 'God' in very large bubble writing.

Bigger, better, bolder, boasting!
(10 minutes)
Explain that this session begins with a game. You need to arrange the group in a circle. Explain that you will start the game off by completing one of the statements from the list below (or one you've made up yourself). The person to your left then has to finish the same statement, but they must make it more outrageous and impressive. Continue round the circle until one of the group can't think of a better boast. At that point, the last person to complete the statement is declared the winner of that round.
- My cat is so clever . . .
- I can run so fast . . .
- My uncle is so rich . . .

(10 minutes)
Watch the film clip from *Harry Potter and the Chamber of Secrets* in which Snape confronts Professor Lockhart about the claims he has been making. Get the group to think about the following questions based on what they have seen.
- What had Lockhart been boasting about? (That he knew where the entrance to the Chamber of Secrets was.)
- Why do you think he'd boasted about this? (To make himself look clever and important.)

- Why did he react in the way he did when Snape called his bluff? (Because he hadn't got a clue where the entrance was and didn't want to appear stupid.)

Big balloon head!

(*10 minutes*)

Give each group member a balloon and a pen. Get them to blow up their balloon as large as they can (without bursting it!) and decorate it to look like a head. Once they've done that, get them to write on their balloon one reason why people boast. Why do people feel the need to make their heads bigger by telling things differently to how they are? Once the young people have finished, go round and share what each person has come up with. When everyone has shared what they have written, they can burst their balloons.

on Bible passage

Bible focus

(*10 minutes*)

Explain to the group that at times we are all guilty of boasting. However, the Bible speaks clearly about when, and about what, it's OK to boast! Get the group to look up Jeremiah 9.23-24 and think about the following questions:

- What things does the passage say people shouldn't boast about? (Being clever or strong or rich.)
- Why do you think God doesn't want us to boast about these sorts of things? (Because they are all things that have been given to us by God – we haven't earned them.)
- So what does the passage says it's OK to boast about? (About knowing God who is kind and just.)

response

God is GREAT!

(*10 minutes*)

Explain that it's often not easy to remember to boast about God! We find it easy to big ourselves up, but we don't find it easy to give God the glory and praise he deserves. Put up the large sheet of paper you prepared before the session, and give each person some Post-it notes and a pen. Leave some time for people to use their Post-it notes to write down words or phrases that show how they feel about God, or things that God has done or given them that they are grateful for – they should write down ways in which they can boast about God, about who he is and what he has done for them. As they write each idea on a new Post-it, get them to stick it on the word 'God' on the sheet of paper. As more people add Post-its, the letters should become covered in the group's boasts. If you run out of space, just put the new Post-its over previous ones. Once everyone has finished writing, end with a prayer of your own or the prayer below.

PLATFORM

9 ³/₄

Dear God,
Help us to boast only about God
about the amazing things he has done
for each and every one of us.
Amen.

6 Right and wrong

SESSION AIM........ **To think about the times when we have to choose between right and wrong**

QUOTATION.......... **Dumbledore:** It is not our abilities that show what we truly are, it is our choices.

FILM FOCUS......... *Harry Potter and the Chamber of Secrets*, chapter 34 (time code: 2:12:27), ending when Malfoy's father enters the room (time code: 2:15:36). (Duration: 3:09)

BIBLE FOCUS........ 'Now, O LORD my God, you have made your servant king in place of my father David. But I am only a little child and do not know how to carry out my duties. Your servant is here among the people you have chosen, a great people, too numerous to count or number. So give your servant a discerning heart to govern your people and to distinguish between right and wrong.' (1 Kings 3.7-9)

RESOURCES.......... *Chamber of Secrets DVD, prepared strips of paper, Bible, A4 paper, green and red pens*

- Photocopy enough copies of the statements included on page 18 to give one set to each group of three or four young people. You will also need a few blank strips of paper for each group.

CORRECT!
(10 minutes)

As you begin the activity, give each young person a piece of A4 paper. Go round one by one and ask each young person a general knowledge question (you could use some of the questions below). If they get the question right, draw a big tick on their piece of paper. If they get it wrong, draw a big cross on their paper. Once everyone has answered a question and has been marked either right or wrong, get everyone to hold up their piece of paper. Explain that in today's session we are thinking about getting things right and getting things wrong. Sometimes working out what's right and what's wrong can be easy, but often when we are faced with a choice, working out the right and wrong decision can be painfully hard.

- How many strings does a normal guitar have? (Six)
- What kind of food is a Stroganoff? (Meat stew)
- Where would you find your Achilles tendon? (Ankle)
- What do we call the only star in our galaxy? (Sun)
- How many wheels does a unicycle have? (One)
- What's Ron Weasley's eldest brother called? (Percy)
- What is glass made from? (Sand)
- What is the capital of Portugal? (Lisbon)
- How many minutes are there in four hours? (240)

(10 minutes)

Watch this session's film clip in which we see Harry talking to Dumbledore, and get your group to think about the following questions:

- What was Harry worried about? (He was worried about the similarities between himself and Tom Riddle.)

- Why did the hat put him in Gryffindor? (He asked the hat to put him in Gryffindor rather than Slytherin.)
- Why did he make that choice? (He didn't want to be part of a house with such negative associations. He wanted to be part of a house that encouraged more positive attributes.)

One or the other
(15 minutes)

Some choices are easy to make – there is clearly a right way and a wrong way. Sometimes the right way is obvious to almost everyone, while at other times the right way is a personal preference which will change from person to person. However, sometimes the right and the wrong choices seem muddled – it's hard to work out which is which. Divide the young people into groups of three or four and give each group a set of the strips of paper you prepared before the session. In their groups, get the young people to put the strips into two piles – the ones where it is easy to decide between right and wrong, and the ones where right and wrong isn't so clear. Make sure they have some blank strips to add their own ideas to the piles. Once the groups have had time to sort the strips, feed back to the rest how each group divided them. In which situations did the young people think that it would be difficult to tell right from wrong?

on Bible passage

Bible focus
(10 minutes)

Explain to the young people that today's Bible verses come shortly after God has told King David's son, a young man called Solomon, that he is going to be king. God promises to give Solomon anything he asks for, and these verses record what Solomon asked for. Read the verses and get the young people to think about the questions below:
- What was worrying Solomon about becoming king? (He was young, he didn't know how to carry out a king's duties, he would be ruling over lots of people.)
- What gift did he ask God for? (The ability to work out right from wrong.)
- Why do the young people think that Solomon thought that this was the best gift he could have asked for? (As king, he would have to make lots of important decisions and this gift would make this task easier.)

response

Green: Start. Red: Stop
(10 minutes)

Reassure the young people that always doing the right thing is difficult – none of us will get it right all the time, but we can keep working at it, and, like Solomon, we can ask God to help us. Give each person a piece of paper and put a selection of red and green pens in the middle of the group. Ask them to write a prayer using the pens. If they want to write a prayer asking God to help them start doing something they know is right, they should use a green pen. If they want to write a prayer asking God to help them stop doing what they know is wrong, they should use a red pen. Emphasize that this is a private activity – they won't be asked to share their prayers with anyone else. Once everyone has written all they want to, finish with a prayer of your own or use the one below.

PLATFORM

Dear God,
Help us to know what is right and what is wrong.
Help us always to choose to do what is right.
Amen.

Photocopy this page onto paper and cut into strips so that you have enough to give one complete set of strips to a group of three or four young people.

Which trainers to buy

Which films to watch and which not to watch

Who to hang around with or not to hang around with

What to look at on the Internet or what not to look at

What chocolate to buy

Which subjects to take at school

Which parties to go to or not go to

Which jokes to tell or not tell

Which gossip to share

Which words to use or not use

7 Stressed

SESSION AIM......... **To think about how we should act when we get stressed**

QUOTATION.......... **Harry:** Shut Up, Shut Up.

FILM FOCUS......... *Harry Potter and the Prisoner of Azkaban*, chapter 2 (time code: 0:01:32), ending when Dudley goes back to watching the television (time code 0:05:48). (Duration: 4:16)

BIBLE FOCUS........ ''In your anger do not sin'': Do not let the sun go down while you are still angry, and do not give the devil a foothold.' (Ephesians 4.26-27)

RESOURCES.......... *Bottles of fizzy drink, bin bags,* Prisoner of Azkaban *DVD, pens, paper, Bible, strips of paper.*

 **BEFOREHAND**

- Get bottles of fizzy drink ready for the first activity.
- Cut up strips of paper to use in the prayer activity.

 OPENING activity

Fizzed up
(*10 minutes*)
Before the start of this activity you will need five or six bottles of fizzy drink. You may want to do this activity outside, or give each person something to cover their clothes with – a bin bag with holes for their head and arms works well. With the group in a circle, throw one of the bottles to another member of the group who then throws it to someone else, and so on. When you're ready, begin counting down from ten. The group member who is holding the bottle when you get to zero has to open the bottle without spraying the drink everywhere! Repeat this activity a few times to see different techniques for opening the bottle safely. Ask those who opened a bottle how they did it – what was their strategy for not ending up covered in fizz? Explain to the group that sometimes we all get angry and it feels like we're all fizzed up inside.

 **FILM CLIP**

(*10 minutes*)
Watch the clip from the beginning of *Harry Potter and the Prisoner of Azkaban* when Harry finds himself being wound up by his aunt. Get them to think about the following questions:

- What things might have made Harry feel more and more angry? (Being ordered around, watching his aunt being so rude, having to wait on everyone else, hearing lies being told about him, having to do the washing up.)
- What was the first sign that Harry was getting stressed? (He made the glass explode.)
- What finally made Harry snap? (His aunt being rude about his mother.)
- What did Harry do when he lost control? (He made his aunt blow up like a balloon!)

Blood boiling

(10 minutes)

Either as a whole group, or in smaller groups if numbers are large, create a mindmap on paper of things that make members of the group angry. What is it that really gets their blood boiling? Write down as many things as the group can think of. Feed back the young people's ideas to the rest of the group.

on Bible passage

Bible focus

(10 minutes)

Get the young people to look up today's passage, which can be found in Ephesians 4.26-27. Read it through as a group and then think about the following questions:

- Why do you think Paul wrote this to the church in Ephesus? (Maybe he'd heard that people getting angry with each other was causing trouble in the church.)
- What do you think Paul means by 'in your anger do not sin'? (When we get angry we are more likely to do things we'll regret later – things we wouldn't normally do.)
- 'Do not let the sun go down while you are still angry' – what did Paul think they should do instead?
- Why might it be better to sort out whatever's made you angry sooner rather than later?

Ready to unwind!?!?

(10 minutes)

Reassure the young people that everyone gets angry from time to time – it's normal. What's important is how we react to that anger. Get the young people to imagine it as being like a spring. Sometimes things wind us up – they wind the spring up tighter and tighter and tighter, sometimes very slowly, sometimes very quickly. What's important is how we react to that spring getting more and more wound up – do we let it unwind slowly, keeping control, or do we let it spring out? Hand each young person a strip of paper. Give them a few minutes to write a short prayer on the strip asking God to help them with the things that make them angry. When they've written it, get them to coil their papers up tight like a spring. When everyone has finished, say a short prayer – one of your own or the one below.

PLATFORM
9 ¾

Dear God,
Help us to control our anger;
  when we get angry, help us not to do things we will regret.
Amen.

Encourage the young people to take their paper springs home as a reminder.

8 Scared

SESSION AIM........ **To think about what scares us and to remember that God is always with us**

QUOTATION........ **Lupin:** I'm very impressed – it suggests that what you fear the most is fear itself – very wise.

FILM FOCUS........ *Harry Potter and the Prisoner of Azkaban*, chapter 11 (time code 0:37:11), ending when Lupin announces the end of the lesson (time code 0:42:49). (Duration: 5:38)

BIBLE FOCUS........ 'The LORD himself goes before you and will be with you; he will never leave you nor forsake you. Do not be afraid; do not be discouraged.' (Deuteronomy 31.8)

RESOURCES........ Prisoner of Azkaban *DVD, Bible*

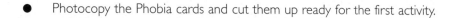

 BEFOREHAND
- Photocopy the Phobia cards and cut them up ready for the first activity.

 OPENING activity

Phobic
(*10 minutes*)
Explain to the group that during this session we will be talking about being scared and that people are scared of very different things. Some people are scared of spiders, while others are scared of much more unusual things! Explain that we're going to play a game – a volunteer will come up, take a phobia card, and then try and mime that phobia. The rest of the group will be told the word for that fear, and will have to try and guess from the volunteer's mimes what this phobia is a fear of.
- Vestiphobia – Fear of clothing
- Trichophobia – Fear of hair
- Ombrophobia – Fear of rain
- Nyctophobia – Fear of night
- Heliophobia – Fear of the sun
- Chronomentrophobia – Fear of clocks
- Xanthophobia – Fear of the colour yellow
- Thaasophobia – Fear of sitting
- Stasibasiphobia – Fear of standing or walking
- Arachibutyrophobia – Fear of peanut butter sticking to the roof of the mouth

 **FILM CLIP**

(*10 minutes*)
Watch this session's clip in which we see Harry's class face some of their fears.
Get the group to talk about the following questions:
- What things are people in the class scared of? (Professor Snape, spiders, snakes)
- What was Harry scared of? (Dementors)

- Why is he scared of them? (He had a bad experience with them earlier in the story.)

Scary stuff

(10 minutes)

Begin by sharing with the group a time from your own life when you were scared by something or of something. It needn't be a hugely personal event from your childhood – it's merely a way of introducing the subject to your young people and showing them that it's OK to be scared of things, even as an adult! Give the young people the chance to share their own stories of times when they have been scared. As you facilitate the young people sharing their stories, make sure that everyone is sensitive to people's stories. Some young people may choose to share events that are particularly emotional for them – make sure that the rest of the group respond appropriately and that they don't ridicule or jest. What is scary for some of us, might appear comical to others! Equally, it might be that your group does not feel they want to share anything – don't panic. Once everyone who wants to has had the chance to talk about a time when they were scared, move on to the next activity.

on Bible passage

Bible focus

(10 minutes)

Reassure them that the Bible is full of scared people – people who were scared of lots of different things. The Bible is also full of the promises God made to those people. One of these promises can be found in Deuteronomy 31.8. Get the group to look up the verse and think about the following questions:
- What promise does God make to us according to this verse? (He will be with us wherever we go, and he will never leave.)
- What do the young people think it means that God will be 'with us' and what do they think this means in reality?
- Why could this promise help us not to be scared? (Whatever happens, whatever we're going through, God is there with us.)
- Do the young people think this means that we'll never be scared at all? (No, there will still be times when we feel scared – but knowing that God is there with us can reassure us.)

response

Wherever you go . . .

(10 minutes)

Explain to the group that there will be times when each and every one of us feels scared, and to know that God is there alongside us, helping us and comforting us, can be very reassuring. This prayer activity is a reminder of this. Ask for a volunteer to stand in the middle of the group, and ask the rest of the group to stand round them in a tight circle, shoulder to shoulder. If you have a larger group of young people, you might want only some of them to form the circle. Ideally, the circle should contain between five and eight young people. It must be very tight – you will see why later on. Tell the person in the middle of the circle to close their eyes and cross their arms across their chest, keeping their feet together. They are then going to fall backwards very gently. The job of the people making the circle is to gently push the person in the middle away using the palms of their hands at shoulder level. The person in the middle will then fall in another direction and will then be pushed in another direction. Because the circle is very tight and the people making it are standing so close together, the person in the middle will never fall very far. Once they have experienced the activity, swap round with a different person in the middle. Obviously this activity requires very careful supervision – you must make sure the circle is tight, and that the young people are being sensible. Also be sensitive to the relative sizes of the people in the circle and the person in the middle. If done properly, this exercise is a great way to get young people to think about God's protection, but if in doubt, stop the activity before it gets out of hand and dangerous! Once everyone's had a chance to be in the middle, finish the session with a prayer – one of your own, or the one below.

Dear God,
Thank you that you will never leave us,
    that you go with us wherever we go.
Help us to know you are near
    especially at those times when we are scared.
Amen.

resource sheet 8 Phobic

Photocopy this page onto paper and cut up into individual cards.

Vestiphobia Fear of clothing	**Trichophobia** Fear of hair
Ombrophobia Fear of rain	**Nyctophobia** Fear of night
Heliophobia Fear of the sun	**Chronomentrophobia** Fear of clocks
Xanthophobia Fear of the colour yellow	**Thaasophobia** Fear of sitting
Stasibasiphobia Fear of standing or walking	**Arachibutyrophobia** Fear of peanut butter sticking to the roof of the mouth

9 Mercy

SESSION AIM......... **To think about how we can show mercy to the people around us**

QUOTATION.......... **Pettigrew:** Harry – James wouldn't have wanted me killed. Your dad – your dad would have spared me – he would have shown me mercy.

FILM FOCUS......... *Harry Potter and the Prisoner of Azkaban*, chapter 25 (time code 1:30:23), ending after Harry says 'The dementors can have you' (time code 1:32:54). (Duration 2:31)

BIBLE FOCUS........ 'Bear with each other and forgive whatever grievances you may have against one another. Forgive as the Lord forgave you.' (Colossians 3.13)

RESOURCES.......... *Paper, pens,* Prisoner of Azkaban *DVD, Bible, rope*

- Prepare a knotted rope for use in the prayer activity. Make sure the knots are not too tight!

They DESERVED it!
(5 minutes)
Explain to the group that you are going to play a game, but before you start there is something the group must do. Give each young person a piece of paper, and get them to write a forfeit on their paper – something the loser of the game will have to do if they lose. Encourage creativity, but remind them that it's possible they themselves might be the loser! Fold up the pieces of paper, and collect them in. Once this is done, get pairs of young people to play a short simple game, such as scissor, paper, stone – one that quickly generates a winner and a loser. Once you have a loser, ask them to pick at random one of the forfeits the group wrote earlier. However, at this point, give the person who originally wrote the forfeit the option to make the loser carry out the forfeit, or show mercy and let them off. If they decide to let the loser off, then they are OK, otherwise they must carry out their forfeit. Repeat the game several times, giving different people the chance to decide the fate of the loser. Do they make the losers carry out the forfeit or do they let them off?

(10 minutes)
Watch this session's clip from *Harry Potter and the Prisoner of Azkaban*. Get the group to talk about the questions that arise from the clip:
- What had Pettigrew done that angered Sirius? (He had betrayed Harry's parents.)
- Why do you think Harry's dad would have wanted Harry to show mercy? (Because he wouldn't have wanted his friends to be killers.)
- Do you think Pettigrew deserved mercy? (No)
- Why did Harry decide not to let Sirius kill him? (Because he decided to act how he knew he ought to – not to let his anger take control of him.)
- Did Harry let Pettigrew get away with what he had done? (No – he planned to hand him over to the dementors.)

Mercy?!?!?

(10 minutes)

Make sure the group knows what mercy means. Get the group to talk about why people show mercy. You might discuss why people chose to let the loser off the forfeit in the first game, or why Harry chose to show mercy towards Pettigrew. Tell the group the story of the Unforgiving Servant. It can be found in Matthew 18.23-35. If your group are likely to know the story, instead get them to tell you the story piece by piece. Talk with the group about the motives of the characters – why did the king show mercy, why didn't the servant? What would group members have done in the same position? Mercy can be a difficult concept to understand – encourage discussion on the subject among the young people. It may help to play devil's advocate or to illustrate the discussion with a scenario more relevant to the lives of the young people.

on Bible passage

Bible focus

(10 minutes)

Explain that we will all have occasion to need to show mercy – to forgive those who have wronged us. And that it is at these moments that we have a choice to make. The Bible is very clear about what our choice should be and why – get the group to look up Colossians 3.13 and think about the following questions:

- How does the verse say we should respond to those people who annoy us? (Tolerate them.)
- What about if they do something really bad to us – should we give them what they deserve? (No – we should forgive them and not hold a grudge.)
- Does that mean we should let people wrong us? (No – we shouldn't let people hurt us, but if and when they do, we need to show forgiveness.)
- Why should we show this mercy to other people? (Because God has shown us great mercy and hasn't punished us for all the bad things we've ever done.)

response

Untie it

(5 minutes)

Reassure the group that each and every one of us will have times when we haven't shown or don't show mercy – when we take our revenge rather than showing the forgiveness that God has shown us. We are all going to get it wrong. Fortunately, if we ask him, God will forgive us for those times. Place the knotted rope in the middle of the circle. Get the young people to think of times when they haven't shown mercy – when they haven't put up with the people who annoy them or forgiven those people who have wronged them. In a time of quiet, invite those young people who want to, to come up and untie one of the knots. As they do so, get them, either out loud or in their heads, to ask God to forgive them. Once everyone has been up who wants to, finish with a prayer. You can use one of your own or the one below.

PLATFORM
9¾

Dear God,
Just as you show mercy to us
  over and over again,
Help us to show mercy to those around us.
Amen.

10 Eyes on the prize

SESSION AIM........ **To think about the prize that awaits us in heaven**

QUOTATION.......... **Dumbledore:** Eternal Glory – that is what awaits the student who wins the Tri-Wizard tournament.

FILM FOCUS......... *Harry Potter and the Goblet of Fire*, chapter 6 (time code: 0:18:27), ending when Dumbledore says 'The Tri-Wizard tournament has begun' (time code: 0:21:27). (Duration 3:00)

BIBLE FOCUS........ Therefore we do not lose heart. Though outwardly we are wasting away, yet inwardly we are being renewed day by day. For our light and momentary troubles are achieving for us an eternal glory that far outweighs them all. So we fix our eyes not on what is seen, but on what is unseen. For what is seen is temporary, but what is unseen is eternal. (2 Corinthians 4.16-18)

RESOURCES.......... *Materials to make an obstacle course, Goblet of Fire DVD, Bible, card, scissors, stapler, pens*

- Set up an obstacle course with a prize at one end. You will need to make the course fairly tricky. It may be that when you come to explain it to the group, they have to do the whole thing without touching the ground or while carrying a full cup of water, etc. BUT, make sure it's safe!
- Photocopy onto card enough copies of the crown template on page 29 to give one to each young person.

In the way!
(*10 minutes*)
Divide the young people into small teams and show them the obstacle course they are going to negotiate as a team. Remind the group of the safety instructions – it may be that each group needs some 'spotters' to walk alongside those doing the obstacle course, making sure they don't fall off. Get the teams to compete to complete the obstacle course and claim the prize at the end.

(*10 minutes*)
Watch the clip from the final part of *Harry Potter and the Goblet of Fire*. Get the group to talk about the following questions:
- What is the prize for winning the Tri-Wizard tournament? (Eternal Glory).
- What do they have to do to win the prize? (Compete in the tournament and survive three dangerous and difficult tasks.)
- Do you think the students will focus on the prize or the difficulties and dangers they will have to face in order to win it? (The prize!)
- Why? (They will be remembered for winning the prize long after the competition is over.)

A victor's prize

(10 minutes)

In pairs, get the young people to come up with ideas of what 'eternal glory' would involve for them. What would be the most amazing celebration of a success or victory? How would they celebrate, who would be there, what would they do etc. Give pairs five minutes to come up with the most impressive and amazing celebration. Once everyone has thought of an idea, share each person's idea of what eternal glory would be like.

on Bible passage

Bible focus

(10 minutes)

Get the young people to look up Paul's thoughts about eternal glory. Get them to discuss the following questions:

● What do you think life was like for Paul as he wrote this? (Difficult – he talks about wasting away and momentary troubles.)

● How is he taking this? (He's remaining positive – he encourages the people he is writing to, not to lose heart.)

● What's keeping him going – what's he focusing on? (An eternal glory that outweighs everything.)

● What do the young people think this eternal glory must be like? (It's worth enduring anything and everything for.)

● Why does Paul tell us it's worth focusing on this unseen eternal glory rather than the troubles they are enduring at the moment? (Because the troubles will end soon, whereas this eternal glory will last forever.)

response

Crown of glory

(10 minutes)

Explain to the young people that later on in the Bible Paul talks about how those people who have fixed their eyes on this unseen goal will one day wear the 'crown of glory' (1 Peter 5.4). To make your own crowns, give each person one of the crown template cards and some scissors. Get the young people to cut down the zigzag, cutting the card into two separate pieces. Staple these two pieces together at 'A' to make one long piece with a flat bottom and a zigzag top – this is the basis of your crown. Give the young people pens and pencils and encourage them to write a prayer on their crown asking God to help them focus on this unseen eternal glory rather than on our own temporary troubles. Once they have written their prayer and decorated their crown (if they wish), staple the other ends of the card together, making sure the crown is the right shape for the young person's head. Finish the session with a prayer of your own or use the one below:

Dear God,
Help us not to lose heart as we seek the eternal glory you promise us. Renew us each day, and help us to overcome the problems we face. Amen.

10 crown of glory

Photocopy this page onto card so that you have enough to give one to each young person.

A
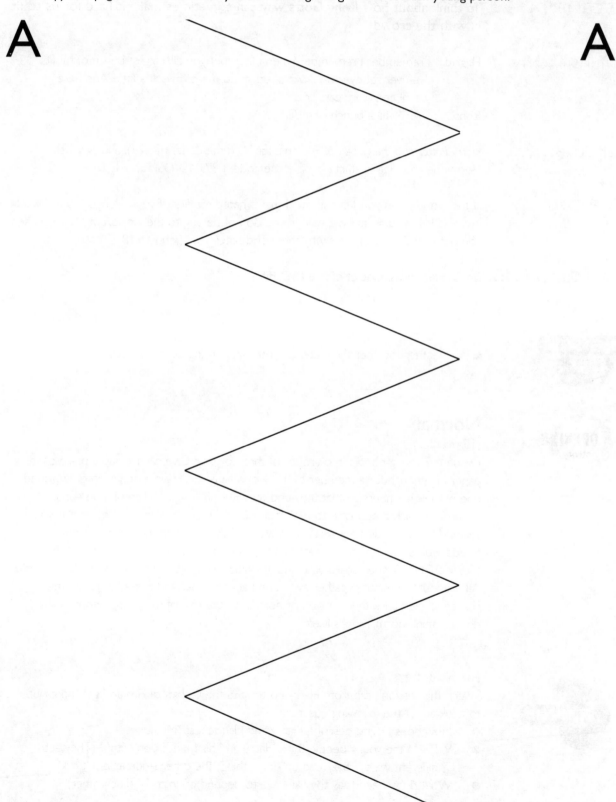
A

11 fitting in

SESSION AIM......... **To think about how living God's way can sometimes make it hard for us to fit in with the crowd**

QUOTATION........... **Hagrid:** I remember, I remember when I first met you all. Biggest bunch of misfits I've ever set eyes on. Always reminded me of myself a little. And here we all are, four years later.

Ron: We're still a bunch of misfits.

FILM FOCUS......... *Harry Potter and the Goblet of Fire*, chapter 20 (time code: 1:35:24), ending when Hermione and Hagrid start singing (time code: 1:37:04). (Duration: 1:40)

BIBLE FOCUS........ 'If the world hates you, keep in mind that it hated me first. If you belonged to the world, it would love you as its own. As it is, you do not belong to the world, but I have chosen you out of the world. That is why the world hates you.' (John 15.18-19)

RESOURCES.......... *Lining paper, pens,* Goblet of Fire *DVD, Bible*

• Gather together the materials you will be using during the session.

Normal
(15 minutes)
Divide the young people into groups of three or four. Give each group a piece of lining paper big enough for a member of the group to lie on. Have each group draw round one of their members so that they end up with the rough outline of a person on their paper. Give each group time to turn their outline into a drawing of a 'normal' twelve-year-old. What would they wear, what would they have with them. Groups might want to add words round their drawing to tell you what music they would listen to, what they would do in their spare time and anything else typical of a normal twelve-year-old. After about ten minutes, gather everyone back together and give each group the chance to feed back their version of 'normal' to the rest of the young people. What do they think 'normal' looks like?

(10 minutes)
Watch this session's clip from Harry Potter and the Goblet of Fire and get the group to think about the following questions:
• How does Hagrid describe Harry and his friends? (Misfits)
• Why do the young people think Harry and his friends don't fit in? (They act in different ways – they end up doing things the other students don't do.)
• What does Hagrid say they all have to depend on instead? (Each other)

Fitting in
(10 minutes)

Everyone wants to fit in, to be like everyone else, to be part of the gang – reassure the group that this is a natural feeling. However, from time to time living as a Christian means we have to make choices or do things that are different from those around us, that make us stand out. Back in the groups they were in for the first activity, using a different coloured pen, get the young people to add to their paper examples of areas of their lives in which acting like God would want them to act would make them appear different from those around them. They might include things such as whether or not to cheat on homework, or whether or not to watch a film their parents told them they couldn't watch. Feed back the ideas each group comes up with. In which areas of their lives might they find it hard to fit in when they are acting as God wants?

on Bible passage

Bible focus
(10 minutes)

Get the group to look up today's Bible passage, in which we see Jesus addressing the difficulties the disciples were having fitting in with the people around them. Think about the following questions:

- Hate is a very strong word. What do you think Jesus meant by it? How did others treat the disciples? (They excluded them, they may even have threatened them.)
- What were the disciples doing that made people treat them in this way? (They were trying to live their lives like Jesus.)
- Why did this anger or worry the people around them? (Because it made the disciples stand out – they didn't fit in and this worried the people around them.)
- Can the young people think of examples of how living their lives as God wants can make them stand out?
- How do the young people think the disciples responded to the news that it was quite likely that some of the people around them were going to hate them for doing what they were doing? What would they have rather Jesus said?

Part of the gang
(5 minutes)

Not fitting in can feel very unpleasant at times – it can be really hard. Emphasize to the young people that this is one of the huge advantages of coming to a group like this – it's a place where they will always fit in, and one where the other members know how hard fitting in among our other friends can sometimes be. Part of the support within the group can come from praying for each other. Go round the group asking each person if they have anything they would like to pray about. Keep a list of what each person asks for. Once everyone has said what they would like to pray for, ask each person to pray for the person on their left, praying for the things that have been asked for. Finish with a prayer of your own or the prayer below.

PLATFORM 9 3/4

Dear God,
You know how hard it can be to fit in among our friends.
Help us to know when to act differently
    and help us when we do.
Amen.

12 Getting lost

SESSION AIM........ **To think about the way God can guide us as we make our way through life**

QUOTATION.......... **Dumbledore:** In the maze you'll find not dragons or creatures of the deep. Instead you'll face something more challenging. You see, people change in the maze. Oh find the cup if you can, but be very wary, you could just lose yourselves along the way.

FILM FOCUS......... *Harry Potter and the Goblet of Fire*, chapter 23 (time code: 1:45:47), ending when the maze closes behind Harry (time code: 1:48:37). (Duration 3:10)

BIBLE FOCUS........ 'I will instruct you and teach you in the way you should go; I will counsel you and watch over you.' (Psalm 32.8)

RESOURCES.......... *Materials to make a path*, Goblet of Fire *DVD, lining paper, pens, Bible, arrows*

- If you have sufficient space, set up the path used during the first activity. Otherwise, prepare a large maze to put on the wall of your venue.
- Draw a path along the middle of a roll of paper. (Lining paper works very well for this activity and is very cheap to buy.)
- Photocopy onto card enough 'arrows' to give one to each young person.

Right a bit ... Left a bit ...
(15 minutes)

If you have sufficient space, set up a path on the floor using rope or chalk, etc. Get the young people into pairs and, one pair at a time, blindfold one of the pair. Their task is to navigate their way along the path you have laid out, deviating as little as possible from the correct route. The job of the other young person in the pair is to shout instructions to their partner. They can't physically guide their blindfolded partner, but they can give as detailed and as frequent instructions as possible. Only one pair at a time should attempt the task and **care should be taken to make sure the young person is safe while blindfolded.** Which pair can navigate the course with the fewest mistakes?

If the venue in which you meet does not suit this activity, draw out a large maze on some paper and stick it to the wall of your venue. Again, divide the young people into pairs and, one pair at a time, blindfold one of the pair and position them in front of your maze. Give the blindfolded young person a pen – their task is to successfully draw a route through the maze. The other young person's job is to give them instructions on where to draw their route. Again, the winning pair are the ones who can navigate the course with the fewest mistakes.

(*10 minutes*)

Explain that sometimes life can be a bit like a maze – there is a path we should follow, a route that's best for us to take. However, the difficulties come when we have to work out where that path is. Watch today's clip in which Harry finds himself having real difficulties navigating his way through a maze. Get the group to think about the following questions:

- How does the crowd feel about the contestants entering the maze? (They are excited.)
- How do the contestants feel about entering the maze? (Nervous)
- What kind of place does the maze look like?
- Why do the young people think that the maze is hard to navigate? (It all looks the same – no one way looks different to any other.)
- Is the maze a safe place? (Possibly not – there are staff available to help if necessary.)
- Where are they trying to get to? (The middle to get to the prize.)

Along the way

(*10 minutes*)

Lay the large roll of paper you've prepared on the floor along the centre of the room in which you meet. Explain to the young people that the piece of paper represents a person's journey through life, with the start at one end, and the end at the other. Give each young person a pen and get them to add to the paper, ideas of times during a person's life when they have to make big choices – when they have to decide which path to take through the maze of life. Encourage them to think about choices they've already had to make and choices they'll have to make in the future, and add them at the appropriate point on life's journey. Once everyone's had a chance to add all the ideas they've come up with, get everyone to sit down, and review the choices people have identified. What are the big choices people have to make during their lives?

FOCUS

on Bible passage

Bible focus

(*10 minutes*)

The Bible has a lot to say about the way in which God is there for people when they have to make difficult choices – the way in which he helps guide them through the maze of life. Have a look at one such instance in the Psalms and think about the following questions:

- What will God do to help us work our way through life's difficult decisions? (He will show us which way we should go.)
- How do the young people think he does this?
- Will God always choose the path that is best for us? (Yes – the verse says he is watching over us.)
- Do we have to choose the path God shows us? (No – he only teaches and counsels, he doesn't MAKE us.)

PRAYER

response

Which way?

(*10 mins*)

Give each young person an 'arrow' and, in a time of quiet, encourage them to write down on one side of the arrow, decisions or questions in which they would like God to help them know which way to go. Encourage them to do this activity quietly as they are honest about the areas of their lives in which they need God's guidance. Once they have done this, get them to write out today's Bible verse on the other side of the arrow as a reminder of the promise that God makes to everyone. Finish the activity with a short prayer of your own, or the one below:

Dear God,
When we have to make difficult and important decisions,
  help us to know which way to go.
Guide us as we make our way through life's maze.
Amen.

Photocopy this page onto paper or card and cut it up so that you end up with enough to give one to each young person.

Mixing it Up!

Liked this one?
Try these!

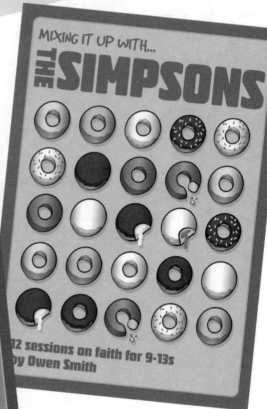

Mixing it up with... The Simpsons
£8.99   978 0 7151 4104 5

Mixing it up with... Football
£8.99   978 0 7151 4105 2

Same author.
Same style.
Different theme.